WE·THE PEOPLE

H O U G H T O N   M I F F L I N

Let's Read

Biography

HOUGHTON MIFFLIN • Boston
Atlanta • Dallas • Geneva, Illinois • Palo Alto • Princeton

WE·THE PEOPLE

HOUGHTON MIFFLIN

Let's Read
Biography

Printed in the U.S.A.

ISBN: 0-395-80627-5

456789 VH 99 98 97

Photography Credits—

Cover and Title Page: *Left to Right from Top to Bottom*
The Granger Collection, New York; ©Sygma; University of Texas/LBJ School of Public Affairs; The Granger Collection, New York; (detail) National Portrait Gallery, Smithsonian Institution/Art Resource, NY; (detail) National Portrait Gallery, Smithsonian Institution/Art Resource, NY; The Granger Collection, New York; Owen Franken/Gamma; ©Photoreporters.

AP/Wide World Photos, v(b); The Bettmann Archive, vi(r); ©Robert Frerck/Odyssey Productions/Chicago, v(t); Owen Franken/Gamma, ii(br), vi(bl); The Granger Collection, New York, ii(tl)(tr), iii(tl), v(tl)(br), vi(t)(cr); The MIT Museum, vi(b); (detail) National Portrait Gallery, Smithsonian Institution/Art Resource, NY, ii(bl), iii(bl), vi(tr)(cl); ©Photoreporters, ii(c), vi(br); Donovan Reese/Tony Stone Images, ii–iii(bkg); ©Sygma, iii(tr), v(cr); University of Texas/LBJ School of Public Affairs, iii(br), v(cl).

Eleanor Roosevelt
Bettmann, 16(r); The Bettmann Archive, 5(b); Franklin D. Roosevelt Library, 2, 4; The Granger Collection, New York, 1, 5(t), 8(t), 11(b), 12, 14(cr)(bl); Thomas McAvoy/*Life Magazine* ©Time Warner, Inc., 9; PhotoDisc Images ©1995 PhotoDisc, Inc., 11(t), 14(t); UPI/Bettmann, 3, 6–7, 7, 8(b), 10, 13, 15, 16(l).

Christa McAuliffe
AP/Wide World Photos, 20(t), 24–25, 31(t); The Bettmann Archive, 19, 21, 26(b); ©Mike Brown/Liaison International, 32(t); ©Gamma Liaison, 27(b); NASA, 30, 31(cr), 32(c); ©Ruben Perez/Sygma, 20(b), 25; ©Sygma, 17, 22, 27(t); UPI/Bettmann, 18, 23, 24, 26(t), 28, 32(b).

Barbara Jordan
AP/Wide World Photos, 40(t), 42, 44(t), 47(br); Archives Division-Texas State Library, 34(tr), 36, 37, 39(tr), 44(b), 47(tr), 48(tr); Bettmann, 41; ©Cynthia Johnson/The Gamma Liaison, 47(bl); LBJ School of Public Affairs, University of Texas at Austin, María de la Luz Martínez, 43(b); ©Bill Malone/Archives Division-Texas State Library, 39(b); PhotoDisc Images ©1995 PhotoDisc, Inc., 46, 47(bkg); ©Photoreporters, 45(tr); ©Tony Stone Images, 45(br); ©Sygma, 33; Texas Southern University, The Barbara Jordan Archives, 34(b), 35; UPI/Bettmann, 40(b), 48(br)(b); UPI/Bettmann Newsphotos, 38, 43(t), 48(cr).

Benito Juárez
AP/Wide World Photos, 64; ©Brian Atkinson/Tony Stone Images, 52–53; The Bettmann Archive, 54(l); Biological Photo Service, 50(br); Corbis-Bettmann, 56(l), 58; ©Robert Frerck/Odyssey Productions/Chicago, 53, 55, 59, 60, 62(b); The Granger Collection, New York, 49, 50(l), 52(cl), 56(r); ©Spencer Grant/FPG International Corp., 63(t); ©Jeremy Horner/Tony Stone Images, 50–51; PhotoDisc Images ©1995 PhotoDisc, Inc., 54(r), 62(tl); ©PhotoEdit, 63(b); ©Porterfield/Chicker/Photo Researchers, Inc., 57(b); ©Stock Montage, 58–59; ©Brenda Tharp/Photo Researchers, Inc., 57(t).

Contents

Eleanor Roosevelt **1**

"First Lady of the World"

Christa McAuliffe **17**

Teacher and astronaut

Barbara Jordan **33**

A woman of firsts

Benito Juárez **49**

"Father of Mexico"

Frederick Douglass . . **65**

Fighter for freedom

Abraham Lincoln 81
Defender of a nation

Benjamin Franklin 97
Inventor, writer, leader

I. M. Pei 113
Designer of great buildings

Antonia Novello 129
Surgeon General—first woman

Eleanor Roosevelt
First Lady of the World

"You must do the thing you think you cannot do."

Early Years

Eleanor Roosevelt was born in New York City on October 11, 1884. Eleanor was not a happy child. She was plain and shy, and she spent much of her time alone or with servants.

Eleanor's parents had died by the time she was ten years old. She and her brother lived with their grandmother, who had many strict rules.

Eleanor was fond of horses, but not of long stockings and high shoes.

At School

Eleanor was sent away to school in England. For the first time, she had friends. Eleanor discovered how exciting learning could be and that helping others was important.

Eleanor at fifteen

Eleanor returned to New York when she was eighteen. She began to spend time with a distant cousin, Franklin Delano Roosevelt. They fell in love and were married.

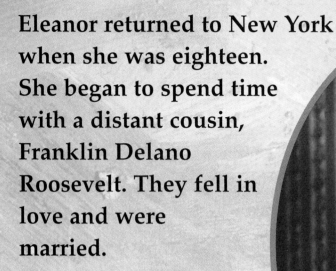

The Roosevelt family

While Franklin was at work, Eleanor cared for her large family. She was surrounded by baby nurses and servants to help her.

Eleanor and her children

Eleanor the Leader

When Franklin went to work in government, Eleanor's life changed. She was interested in meeting and talking with many different people.

Eleanor became a newswoman.

Eleanor traveled all over America and the world. Here she is about to enter a coal mine.

When Franklin was elected president of the United States, Eleanor became the First Lady. Both Eleanor and Franklin believed that government should help people in need.

Franklin D. Roosevelt

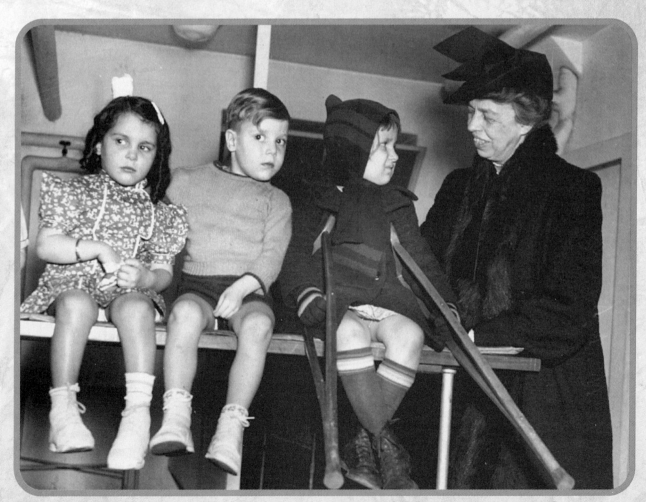

Eleanor cared about people. Here she visits children at a hospital.

Eleanor had the courage to stand up for what she believed. The Daughters of the American Revolution would not allow Marian Anderson, a great singer, to perform in their concert hall because she was African American. Eleanor gave up her membership in the group in protest.

Eleanor invited Marian Anderson to sing in front of the Lincoln Memorial.

On December 7, 1941, the United States entered the Second World War. Eleanor traveled around the world to visit American soldiers.

Eleanor visiting a United States aircraft carrier

After Franklin's death, Eleanor became part of the United States group at the United Nations. There she worked with other leaders for peace.

Eleanor is shown here answering news reporters' questions.

Eleanor was a strong speaker, and she wrote a daily newspaper article. She was admired by people around the world.

Eleanor died on November 7, 1962 at the age of seventy-eight. At her funeral, President Harry S. Truman called her "First Lady of the World."

This photo was taken the year before Eleanor died.

Let's Explore!

Hyde Park, the home of the Roosevelts, is now a national park. What are some of the places to visit there?

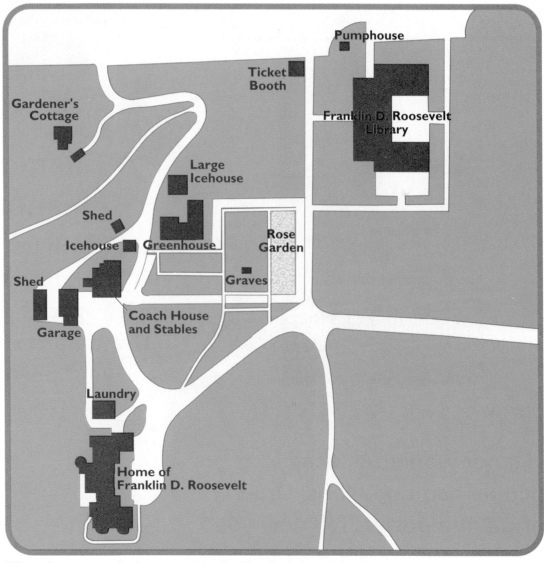

The Roosevelt home, Hyde Park, New York

What Do You Think?

How I Help Others

Eleanor helped many people. List ways you help others. Then use your list to write a story about helping someone. Share your story.

MAKE A POSTER

Eleanor worked so that people had good jobs. Draw or paint a poster. Tell why you want good jobs for everyone.

A Poem for Eleanor

Write a poem telling why you think Eleanor was such a special person. Draw a picture for your poem.

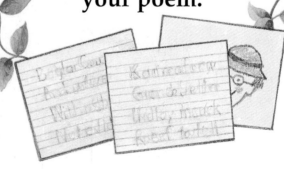

OTHER FIRST LADIES

Jacqueline Kennedy Onassis won praise for making the White House a historic showplace for visiting dignitaries and tourists alike.

Lady Bird Johnson won recognition for sponsoring projects aimed at the beautification of interstate highways and the District of Columbia.

Nancy Reagan sponsored activities that targeted drug and alcohol abuse in young people, becoming famous for her "Just say no!" to drugs campaign.

Barbara Bush understood the importance of learning to read and helped start the Barbara Bush Foundation for Family Literacy.

Key Events

1884	Born in New York City on October 11
1899	Sent to school in England
1905	Married Franklin Delano Roosevelt
1933-1945	Was First Lady of the United States
1942	Visited soldiers during the war
1945	Appointed to the United Nations
1962	Died on November 7

At the 1940
Democratic Convention

Christa McAuliffe

NASA (National Aeronautics and Space Administration) wanted to send a teacher into space. Sharon Christa McAuliffe was the first teacher to be chosen. Christa didn't want to be an astronaut though. She wanted to teach children about space.

Christa with some of her students

In 1948 Christa McAuliffe was born in Framingham, Massachusetts. As a young girl, she loved school, music lessons, Girl Scouts, and sports. She wanted to be a teacher when she grew up.

As an adult, Christa taught social studies to high-school students.

Christa studied to be a teacher. She married her husband, Steven, just after she finished college.

Christa and Steven with their children, Scott and Caroline

After college Christa's life was busy raising two children and teaching social studies at a high school in New Hampshire. She believed that each student learned best by doing activities and seeing things in person.

Christa's excitement in her classroom carried over to her training.

Then Christa heard about a search for a teacher to go into space. Steve told Christa to "go for it." Those words changed both their lives.

Christa told her students any dream could come true if they had the courage to work at it.

In order to be chosen, teachers had to tell why they wanted to go into space. Christa didn't apply until just before the deadline.

One of ten finalists, McAuliffe smiles as Vice President George Bush tells her she has been selected.

Many of the teachers who applied for the contest wanted to teach science projects. Christa wanted to keep a journal of her training and record her thoughts. Then she could share her flight with her students. This simple idea helped NASA to choose Christa McAuliffe.

Other teachers congratulate Christa.

NASA chose Sharon Christa McAuliffe on July 19, 1985. She would be the first teacher to travel into space.

Christa at the controls during training

Christa, with Steve, proudly shows her space suit.

Christa had to learn to do simple things in different ways. On Earth gravity pulls us down. In space there is no gravity. Everything can float away. Christa had to learn to eat, sleep, and move in space.

Christa trained every day.

10–9–8–7–6–5–4–3–2–1 Blast off! The rocket that carried the space shuttle *Challenger* was launched on January 28, 1986. Just minutes into the flight, the space shuttle exploded. Christa and all of the astronauts died in the explosion.

The *Challenger* crew:
Front—Michael J. Smith, Francis R. (Dick) Scobee, Ronald E. McNair
Back—Ellison S. Onizuka, Sharon Christa McAuliffe, Gregory Jarvis, Judith A. Resnick

Christa had dreamed of being a teacher. She is remembered and honored as the first teacher in space.

Christa will be remembered as a person who tried hard and did the best she could.

S. CHRISTA McAULIFFE

Let's Explore!

Christa McAuliffe was born in Massachusetts. She taught school in New Hampshire. She trained for her space flight in Texas. She took off on her flight from Florida. Find on the map the cities in which these events happened.

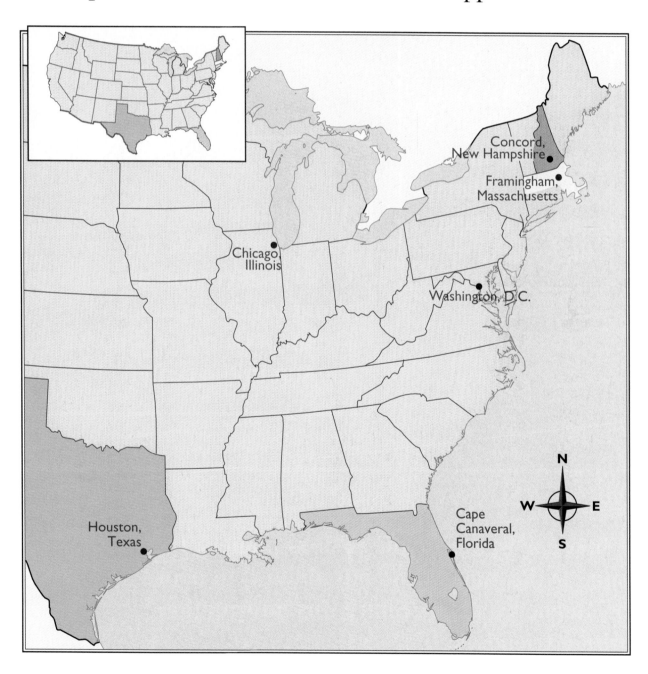

What Do You Think?

My Journal

Christa McAuliffe wanted to keep a journal about her space flight. Keep a journal for a week. Write about what you learn and do during that week.

Planet Mobile

The planets are different sizes. They circle the sun. Color and cut out a circle to stand for each planet. Create a planet mobile with the sun in the center.

Space Report

Choose a "space" topic such as planets, the sun, or the moon. Find out about it in books or an encyclopedia. Share this information with a friend.

THE SPACE SHUTTLE

Look at these photos and diagrams. The space shuttle is big. The shuttle has three levels. Look at where the astronauts sleep.

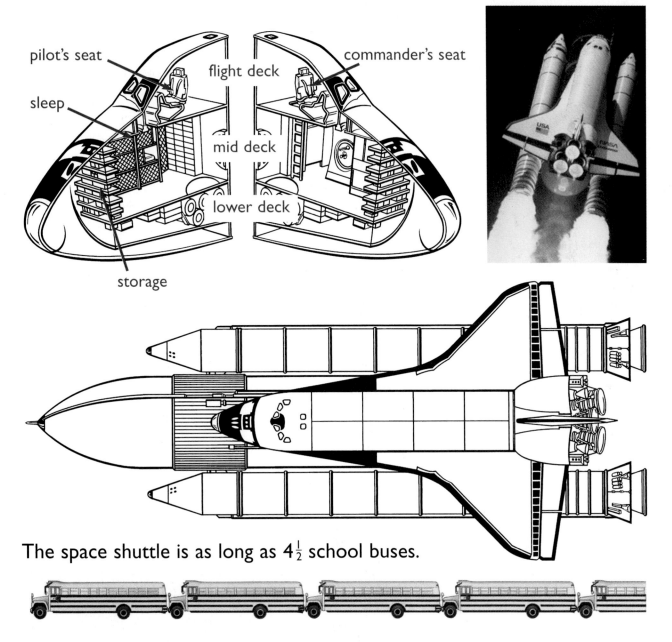

pilot's seat

flight deck

commander's seat

sleep

mid deck

lower deck

storage

The space shuttle is as long as $4\frac{1}{2}$ school buses.

Key Events

1948 Born Sharon Christa Corrigan September 2

1966 Graduated from Marian High School, Framingham, Massachusetts

1970 Graduated from Framingham State College and married Steven McAuliffe

1982 Started teaching at Concord High School

1985 Was first teacher chosen to travel in space

1986 Died aboard the *Challenger* when it exploded

Barbara Jordan

"I don't deal with *ever*. I deal with *now*."

Barbara Jordan

In 1936 Barbara Jordan was born in Houston, Texas. Her parents were poor. They taught Barbara the importance of hard work and education.

Barbara was vice-president of her junior class in college. She's shown here (second from the left) with the other class officers.

Barbara knew that getting a good education was her chance for a better life. She was a fine student who had a talent for debating. In a debate two people discuss reasons for and against something. Barbara won medals for her debates.

Barbara Jordan and a teammate accept a debate trophy.

Barbara joined the debate team in college and traveled all over the country. She graduated from college with honors.

In 1956, Barbara debated with the Harvard University debate team.

After college, Barbara went to law school in Boston. She studied hard and worked long hours.

Barbara worked hard to open her own law office.

Barbara returned to Texas to practice law. She ran for the Texas House of Representatives twice and lost both times. Then she ran for the Texas Senate in 1966, and she won!

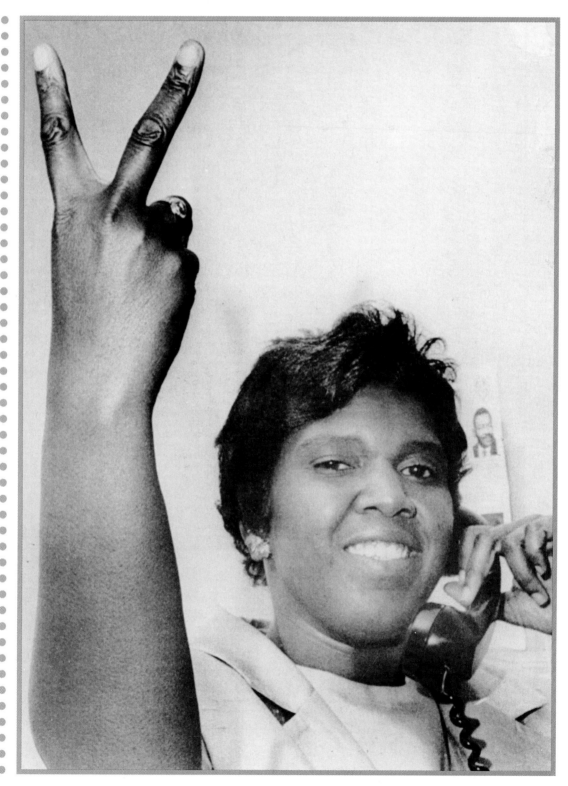

Barbara Jordan flashes the victory sign after winning.

Barbara was a good senator. She fought hard for the people of her district.

Before leaving the Texas State Senate, Barbara was voted governor for a day.

Barbara ran for election to the U.S. House of Representatives and won. She became a respected congresswoman.

Barbara Jordan with
President Gerald Ford

Speaking before the
House of Representatives
committee

Barbara was invited to speak at the Democratic National Convention in 1976. She was the first African American woman ever asked to give the keynote speech at a national convention.

Barbara Jordan was given a standing ovation after her 1976 keynote speech. People cheered and shouted.

Barbara was a congresswoman for six years. She supported many laws that would help all Americans. After serving three terms, Barbara wanted to go home to Texas.

Barbara Jordan received an honorary degree from Harvard University.

Barbara returned to Texas and became a college teacher. She wanted to help young people learn about government.

Barbara Jordan left the House of Representatives after six years.

Professor Jordan expected her students to work hard.

Over the years, many people had hoped Barbara would run for office again. They admired the work she did for others. She has made a place for herself in the history of Texas and of our country.

Barbara Jordan used a wheelchair because of illness. She's shown here at the 1988 Democratic Convention in Atlanta.

President Clinton with Jordan

Let's Explore!

Barbara Jordan was born in Texas. She worked as a representative in Washington, D.C. Point out Washington, D.C. on the map. Tell what direction Washington, D.C., is from Texas.

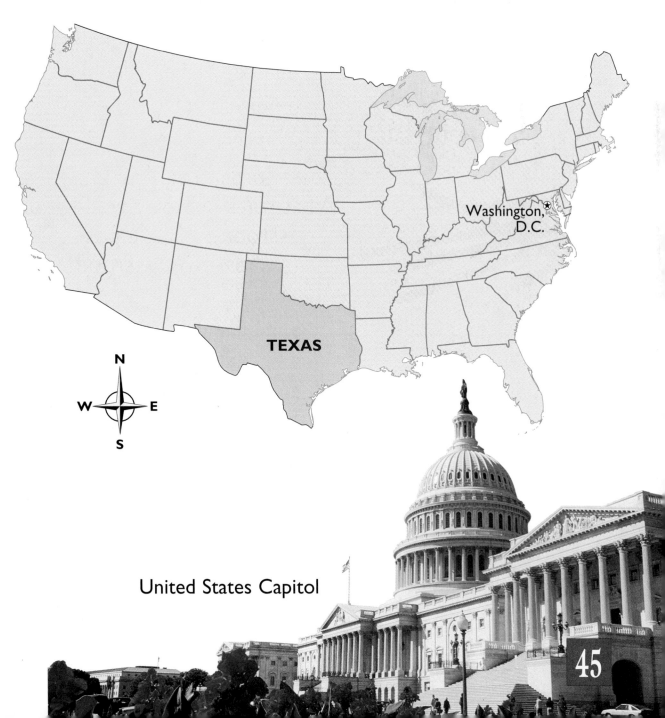

Washington, D.C.

TEXAS

United States Capitol

What Do You Think?

What Do You Want to Be?

Tell about what you would like to be when you grow up. What do you have to learn to meet your goal? Share this information with a friend.

RULES HELP PEOPLE

Barbara Jordan helped make laws. What rules do you have in your classroom? Make a poster to show the classroom rules.

I Can Do It!

Barbara Jordan liked to make speeches. List some things you like to do. Then draw a picture of yourself doing one of the things from your list.

46

A Woman of Firsts

Barbara was the first African American woman elected to the Texas Senate.

Barbara was the first African American woman ever to be governor of a state. As a way of saying good-by, the Texas Senate voted her governor for one day.

Barbara was the first African American woman to give the keynote address at a national convention.

Being sworn in as governor for a day

At the 1992 Democratic National Convention

At the 1976 Democratic National Convention

47

Key Events

1936   Born in Houston, Texas

1959   Received her law degree from
Boston University

1966   Elected Texas state senator

1972   Elected to United States
House of Representatives

1976   Spoke at the Democratic
National Convention

1978   Retired from the House of
Representatives and
became a professor at
University of Texas

1979   Became a professor at
Lyndon B. Johnson School of Public Affairs

1992   Received the Springarn Medal for service in
Congress

1996   Died on January 17

Benito Juárez

I am an Indian and I do not forget my own people.

Benito Juárez

In 1806 Benito Juárez was born in a village in Mexico. His parents were Zapotec Indians. They died by the time Benito was three years old.

Mexican Indians grinding corn and shaping tortillas

Benito lived with his grandfather and then his uncle.
As Benito grew, his days were spent taking care
of his uncle's sheep.

A couple working the land in Oaxaca today

In those times Mexico was ruled by Spain.
Like most people in Benito's village, Benito spoke
only Zapotec. He wanted to learn how to speak
and write Spanish.

In Benito's time, priests often taught the
Mexican Indian children to read Spanish.

When Benito was twelve years old, he left his village. He walked about forty miles to the city of Oaxaca. There he stayed in the home where his older sister was living and working.

This church in Oaxaca was built in the 1500s. It is still standing today.

Benito found a job as a houseboy for a very rich man. The man liked Benito and helped him get into school.

Benito studied law at the Institute of Arts and Sciences.

As he grew, Benito saw how the poor were treated differently than the rich. He knew this wasn't fair. He studied to become a lawyer so he could defend the rights of the poor people.

A house in Oaxaca today

By the time Benito finished school, Mexico had won its independence from Spain. The people in the new government still were not fair to many Mexicans. Juárez worked hard to change that.

Benito Juárez

Antonio Santa Anna

Juárez and Santa Anna fought each other for control of the Mexican government after it won its independence from Spain.

Benito Juárez became governor of the state of Oaxaca.
He built schools and roads. The poor loved him
but the rich did not. Juárez was even forced to
leave Mexico, but he returned.

Oaxaca today

JUAREZ

Juárez became a powerful lawmaker. One of his laws, called the Juárez Law, said that all Mexicans were equal. Many of his ideas were written into the Constitution of 1857.

The constitution brought reforms to Mexico.

Benito Juárez became president in 1858. Armies in Mexico were fighting each other, but President Juárez led his army to victory.

After many struggles, President Juárez returned to Mexico City in triumph.

President Juárez was welcomed to the palace.

Benito Juárez died in his fourth term as president.
To this day, Mexicans honor him as a great hero.

Monuments to honor Benito Juárez, in Mexico City (above) and in Oaxaca (left)

Let's Explore!

Benito Juárez was born in a village near Oaxaca. As president, he lived in Mexico City. Point out Mexico City on the map. Tell which direction Mexico City is from Oaxaca.

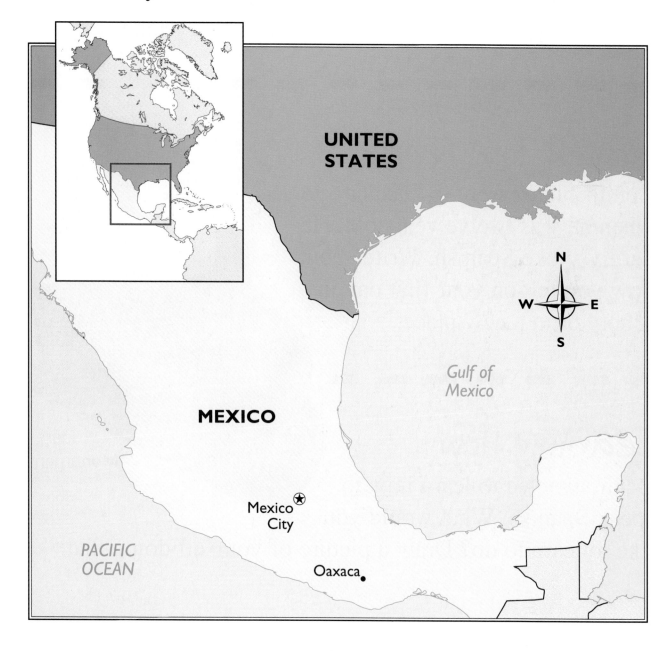

What Do You Think?

Spanish Words

Benito learned Spanish when he was twelve years old. Learn two words in Spanish, such as *hello* and *good-bye*. Use the words with a friend.

Man of the People

Benito Juárez went to Oaxaca when he was twelve years old. He hardly spoke Spanish. Write about how you felt on your first day in school or in a new place.

Juárez Monument

Learning How

Benito wanted to learn how to speak Spanish. What would you like to learn to do? Draw a picture of yourself doing that.

CINCO DE MAYO

On the morning of May 5, 1862, the Mexican army beat the French army at the city of Puebla. Eventually, the Mexicans, under the leadership of Benito Juárez, won their freedom. Every year on May 5th, many Mexicans and Mexican Americans celebrate *Cinco de Mayo*.

Key Events

1806 Born in the state of Oaxaca, Mexico

1818 Went to city of Oaxaca to study

1828 Went to college

1831 Started practicing law in Oaxaca

1843 Married Margarita Maza

1847 Elected governor of the state of Oaxaca

1855 Became Minister of Justice

1858 Became president of Mexico

1872 Died in Mexico City

In 1972, Mexico's ambassador presented a portrait of Benito Juárez to the librarian of the Library of Congress.

Frederick Douglass was born a slave. His real name was Frederick Bailey. He didn't know the date he was born. All he knew was that he was born in February.

Many slaves spent their days picking cotton.

When Frederick was about six, he went to work as a slave on a farm. After several years, his owner sent him to Baltimore. There he worked as a slave for Hugh and Sophia Auld. He took care of Hugh and Sophia's baby.

Slaves could be bought and sold.

Sophia treated Frederick well. She taught the boy to read. When her husband found out, he made her stop. But Frederick kept reading. He even taught himself to write.

Sophia and Frederick

Frederick as a young man

A photograph of Frederick

When Frederick was about sixteen, he worked for a farmer who treated him badly. Frederick had to work in all kinds of weather. He was often too tired to stand at the end of the day.

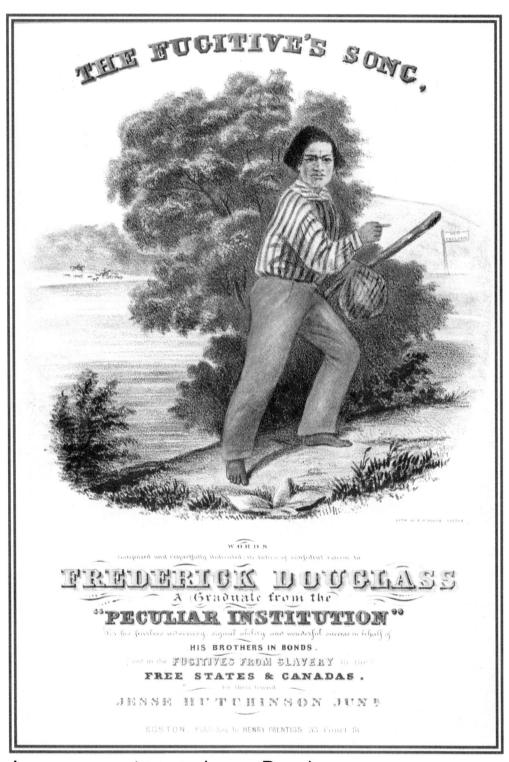

A song was written to honor Douglass.
This is the cover of the song sheet.

One master treated Frederick with kindness, but Frederick wanted to be free. He and some other slaves planned to run away, but Frederick's master found out. Frederick was sent back to Auld.

Back in Baltimore, Frederick worked in a shipyard.

Frederick met and fell in love with Anna Murray. Anna lent him money to run away. In 1838 Frederick escaped to the North. Once there he changed his name to Douglass so he would not be easily captured by slave hunters.

Anna Murray was a free woman who worked for a rich Baltimore family.

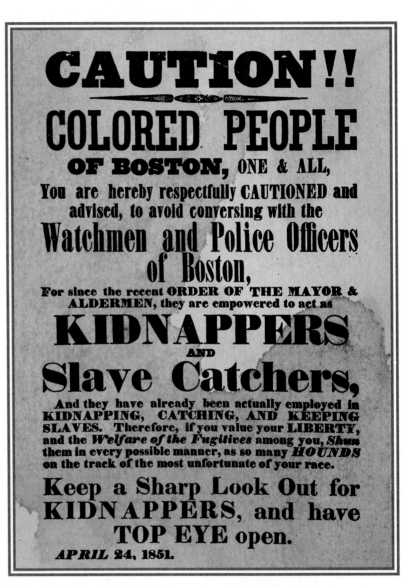

People were paid money to find runaway slaves.

Frederick sent for Anna, and they were married. He told people how bad slavery was. Frederick said that all African Americans should be free. He said they should be able to have the right to vote.

Douglass's speeches about slavery made him famous.

This book was one of the first to tell about the wrongs of slavery.

Frederick's words about freedom made many people want to end slavery. He wrote a book about slavery. Frederick was afraid his old owner would read the book, and then he would know where Frederick was.

Douglass's book became a bestseller.

Douglass, second from the left, helped slaves run away.

Frederick ran away to England. There he became famous for his speeches. He faced the possibility of being caught and sent back into slavery. With help from his English friends, he bought his freedom. He returned to America a free man.

Frederick started his own newspapers. He called one newspaper *The North Star,* after the star that slaves followed to freedom.

Frederick worked for the Union Army during the Civil War. He and President Lincoln talked about the war. They also talked about how all people should be free.

Douglass wanted all people to be free.

After Anna Douglass died, Frederick continued the fight for freedom for everyone. Frederick died when he was seventy-seven years old.

Douglass read many books and was an excellent writer.

Let's Explore!

Frederick Douglass traveled a long way from Maryland to find freedom in the North. Use the map to tell which directions Frederick took as he traveled.

What Do You Think?

DREAMS

Frederick Douglass liked to watch ships sail by when he was young. He dreamed of sailing on a ship. What do you dream of doing? Talk to family members and friends about their dreams. How are your dreams alike? How are they different?

Help Wanted

Frederick Douglass worked for freedom for everyone. Make a poster that shows something you feel strongly about, such as planting trees or saving the whales. Write what your idea is and tell how people can help.

Other Freedom Fighters

Susan B. Anthony

Sojourner Truth

William Lloyd Garrison

Wendell Phillips

Key Events

1818 Born Frederick Bailey in Talbot County, Maryland

1826 Lives as a slave in Baltimore, Maryland

1836 Tries to escape but fails

1837 Meets Anna Murray

1838 Escapes to New York; marries Anna Murray, and changes name to Frederick Douglass

1845 Publishes *Narrative of the Life of Frederick Douglass*

1847 Begins *The North Star*

1863 Meets President Lincoln for the first time

1880 Serves as recorder of deeds in Washington, D.C.

1882 Death of Anna Douglass

1889 Serves as American consul general to Haiti

1895 Dies in Washington, D.C.

ABRAHAM LINCOLN

Lincoln as a Young Boy

This is a story of a great man. It begins in a log cabin in Kentucky. On February 12, 1809, Abraham Lincoln was born.

Lincoln's home looked much like this.

I was born Feb. 12, 1809, in Hardin County, Kentucky.

As a boy, Abe worked hard doing farm chores. He stayed up at night reading books. Abe loved to read and write.

Abe reading by firelight

A page from Lincoln's homemade math book

Lincoln as a Young Man

Abe worked at many jobs. He was a rail-splitter, a storekeeper, and a postmaster. Abe wanted to do more. He wanted to work as a lawmaker in his state of Illinois. When the day came for the people to vote, Abe did not win.

This painting is called
The Rail Splitter.

Abe steering a flatboat
on the Mississippi River

Abe was not a man to give up. A few years later he asked the people again to elect him as a lawmaker. This time he won!

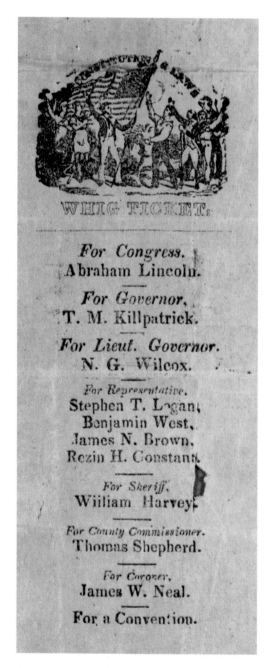

Lincoln belonged to the Whig political party. The ticket lists names from Illinois.

An early photo of Lincoln taken in Illinois

Abe Lincoln the Lawyer

Abe studied to be a lawyer. He became known all around Illinois. Some settlers had problems. They argued about land or animals or money. Abe Lincoln helped them solve their problems.

Abraham Lincoln defending a young man in court

Abe Lincoln the Leader

In 1842 Abe married Mary Todd. It was a time of many changes. Abe wanted to work for his state in the United States Congress. The people of Illinois knew Abraham Lincoln as a fine man who worked hard for his state. They voted for Abe to be their voice in Washington, D.C.

Lincoln with his fourth son Tad

Mary Todd

The nation's people argued about slavery. In some states African Americans were forced to work without pay. Abe thought this was wrong. He asked the people of the United States to vote for him as President.

Objects from Lincoln's campaign

In 1860 Abraham Lincoln was elected President of the United States. The Lincoln family moved into the White House in Washington, D.C.

A terrible war began between the states. As President, Lincoln signed a special law that freed African Americans who were enslaved. Some states did not want to obey the law.

Lincoln wore this hat during the war. He would often keep letters and papers in it.

President Lincoln talking with a general about the war

During the war Abe made a speech that honored all the soldiers who died in the war. After many long years the war finally did end.

Lincoln gave his famous speech at Gettysburg, Pennsylvania. Part of that speech is seen below.

President Lincoln at a battlefield

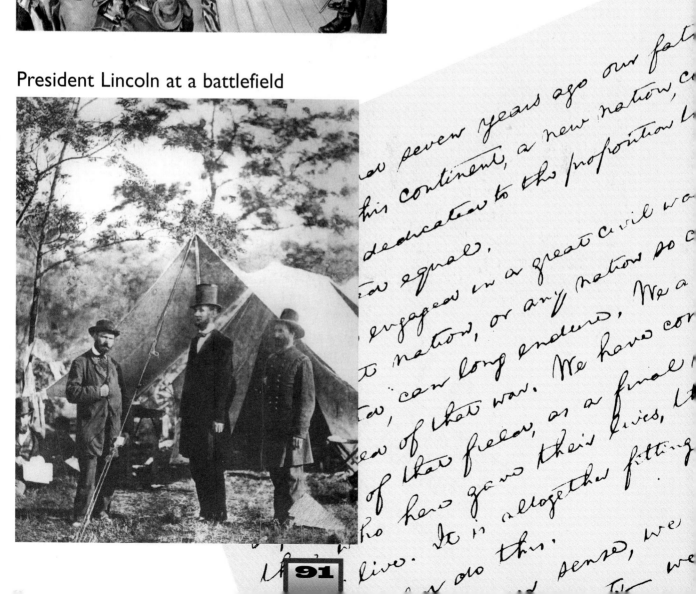

One night Abraham Lincoln went to the theater. He was shot, and later he died. The nation was very sad to lose such a fine leader. Each year on Presidents' Day, we honor the life of Abraham Lincoln. He was a great leader who believed in freedom for all people.

Abraham Lincoln was the sixteenth President of the United States.

Let's Explore!

Read about some events in Abe Lincoln's life. Use the map to see where each event took place.

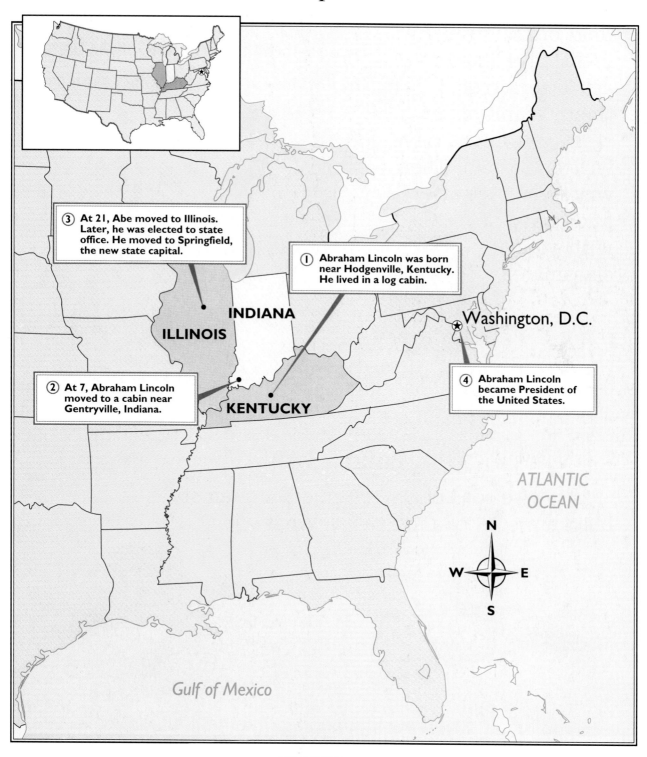

(3) At 21, Abe moved to Illinois. Later, he was elected to state office. He moved to Springfield, the new state capital.

(1) Abraham Lincoln was born near Hodgenville, Kentucky. He lived in a log cabin.

Washington, D.C.

INDIANA

ILLINOIS

(2) At 7, Abraham Lincoln moved to a cabin near Gentryville, Indiana.

(4) Abraham Lincoln became President of the United States.

KENTUCKY

ATLANTIC OCEAN

N
W E
S

Gulf of Mexico

What Do You Think?

Dear Mr. Lincoln

President Lincoln was fond of children. He must have liked to get letters from them. Think about what you might have written to him. Then write your letter and share it with your classmates.

All About Abe

Give a short talk on Abraham Lincoln. Tell what he did as a boy, a young man, and the President of the United States. Draw pictures that show parts of his life.

Build a Cabin

Use rolls of clay or glue and craft sticks to build a model of a log cabin. What will you use for windows and doors?

Honoring Abraham Lincoln

We honor Abraham Lincoln in statues, with monuments, on stamps, and on money.

West Virginia State Capitol

The Lincoln Memorial in Washington, D.C.

Penny

Lincoln stamp

Five-dollar bill

Key Events

1809 Born in Kentucky on February 12

1834 Elected to the Illinois state legislature

1842 Married Mary Todd

1846 Elected to United States House of Representatives

1860 Elected President of the United States

1863 Signed the Emancipation Proclamation to end slavery

1864 Reelected President of the United States

1865 Died on April 15 in Washington, D.C.

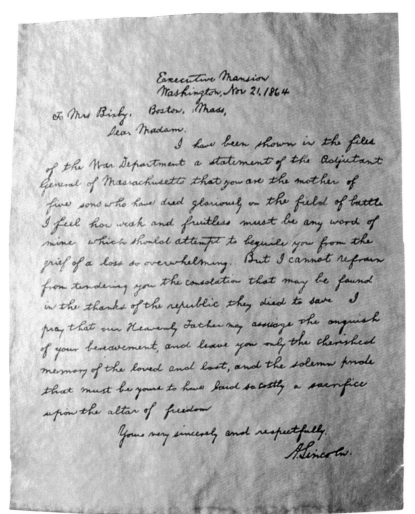

Lincoln was a caring man. He wrote this letter to a mother who lost her five sons in the war.

Benjamin Franklin

A Boy of Invention

The Franklin family lived in Boston, Massachusetts. Ben was born in 1706. He had sixteen brothers and sisters. At that time our country was still a colony—a part of England. As Benjamin grew, so did the country.

FRANKLIN'S BIRTHPLACE.

Ben went to school for only two years. He learned to read and write there. After that, he taught himself many things. Ben had big ideas about how things worked.

When Ben was a man, he did experiments with lightning using a kite and a key.

When Ben was twelve years old, his brother James taught him how to be a printer. Ben learned all about printing newspapers.

Title page of a book about Franklin

Young Benjamin at work

A Young Man of Letters

Ben played a trick on his brother. He wrote letters to his brother's newspaper and signed the letters "Silence Dogood." Many people liked reading the letters in the newspaper, but James was not happy. When he found out Ben had written the letters, he was angry.

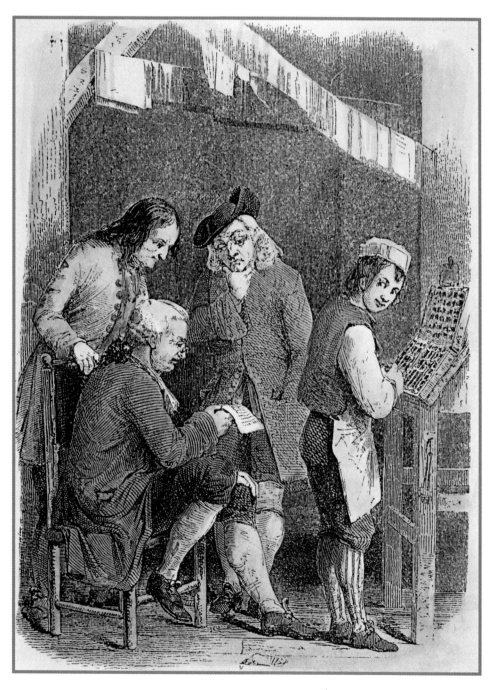

Franklin, far right, working for his brother

101

When Ben was seventeen he went to Philadelphia to find work. Ben worked for printing houses in Philadelphia and in London, England. He was bursting with new ideas and opened his own print shop in Philadelphia. He printed a book each year called *Poor Richard's Almanack*. The book was filled with weather forecasts, advice, and wise sayings.

Franklin started his own print shop. He used a pen name when he wrote *Poor Richard's Almanack*.

Poor Richard, 1733.

AN

Almanack

For the Year of Chrift

1733,

Being the Firft after LEAP YEAR:

And makes fince the Creation	Years
By the Account of the Eaftern *Greeks*	7241
By the Latin Church, when ☉ ent. ♈	6932
By the Computation of *W.W.*	5742
By the *Roman* Chronology	5682
By the *Jewifh* Rabbies	5494

Wherein is contained

The Lunations, Eclipfes, Judgment of the Weather, Spring Tides, Planets Motions & mutual Afpects, Sun and Moon's Rifing and Setting, Length of Days, Time of High Water, Fairs, Courts, and obfervable Days.

Fitted to the Latitude of Forty Degrees, and a Meridian of Five Hours Weft from *London*, but may without fenfible Error, ferve all the adjacent Places, even from *Newfoundland* to South-Carolina.

By RICHARD SAUNDERS, Philom.

PHILADELPHIA:

Printed and fold by *B. FRANKLIN*, at the New Printing-Office near the Market.

Ben arrived in Philadelphia with little money.

Ben the Inventor

Ben had ideas to help people. Fires were very common in cities like Philadelphia. The fires burned many houses. Ben's idea was to set up a fire department.

One artist painted Ben as a firefighter.

Ben Franklin even invented a way to make better use of fire. He created a metal stove that fit inside a fireplace.

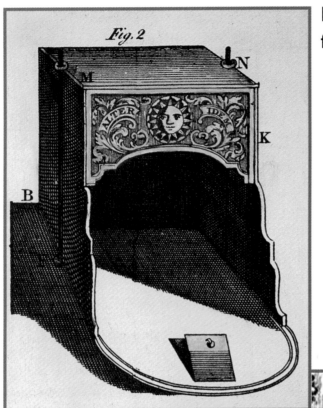

Franklin's design for a stove

The Franklin stove used less wood and threw more heat into a room.

Ben got tired of switching to reading glasses every time he had something to read. So he cut his lenses in half. He put the reading lenses together with regular lenses in one frame.

Franklin invented bifocals.

Lens for looking at things far away

Lens for reading

A National Leader

Many people thought England's rules were unfair. Ben and other leaders wrote their ideas in the Declaration of Independence. They asked the king of England to let the colonies have a say in making rules.

The Declaration of Independence committee, with Franklin at the far left

Franklin presenting the Declaration of Independence

The Declaration led to war between England and the colonies. The colonies needed help to win. Ben had an idea! At 70 years old, Ben sailed across the Atlantic Ocean to ask France for help in the war.

FRANKLIN'S RECEPTION AT THE COURT OF FRANCE 1778.

Benjamin Franklin meeting the king and queen of France

At age 84 Ben Franklin died. His inventions, writings, and many of his good ideas live on today.

Let's Explore!

This map shows Philadelphia when Benjamin Franklin lived there. Tell how Franklin could travel from his house to Independence Hall.

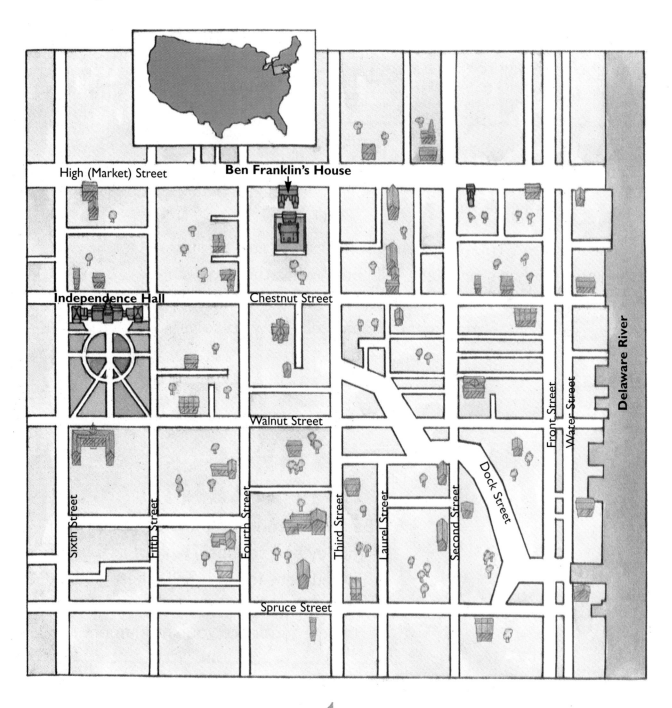

What Do You Think?

BIG IDEAS

Do you have a big idea you think would help others? Share your idea in pictures and words. Your big idea might be a new way to do something that saves time or effort, or it might be a way to solve arguments among your friends.

NO PROBLEM

With a friend, role-play being Ben Franklin and a young friend who has a problem. Tell "Ben" what the problem is, such as your house is cold or you can't read the newspaper. "Ben" tells how to solve the problem.

A FRANKLIN MONUMENT

Benjamin Franklin's picture appears on money and stamps. Think of a monument for him. Tell where you would build it. Then draw a picture or build a model of your monument.

BEN'S SIGNATURE

Benjamin Franklin signed all four of these documents: the Declaration of Independence, the Treaty of Alliance, the Treaty of Paris, and the Constitution of the United States.

Declaration of Independence	Treaty of Alliance	Treaty of Paris	Constitution of the United States
Document that gave the reasons why the colonists wanted their independence	Agreement between France and the colonists	Agreement that ended the war with England	Document that described how the new United States government would work

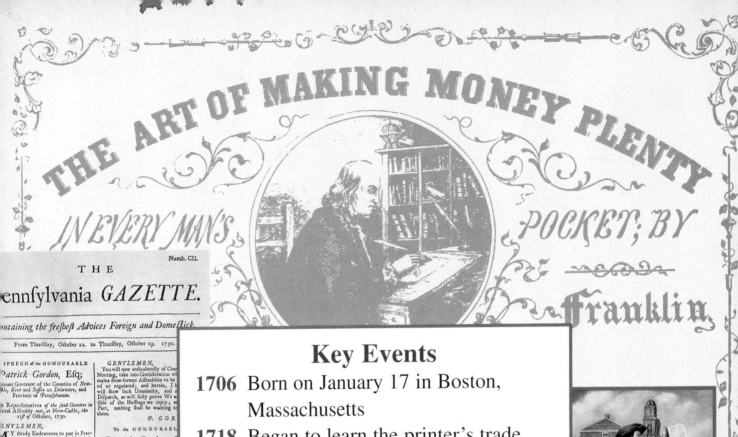

THE ART OF MAKING MONEY PLENTY IN EVERY MAN'S POCKET; BY Franklin

The Pennsylvania GAZETTE.

Key Events

1706 Born on January 17 in Boston, Massachusetts

1718 Began to learn the printer's trade from his brother James

1723 Went to Philadelphia, Pennsylvania

1729-1766 Published *The Pennsylvania Gazette*

1733-1758 Published *Poor Richard's Almanack* each year

1737 Was postmaster for Philadelphia, where he set up a mail delivery system

1752 Used key and kite to experiment with lightning

1776 Signed the Declaration of Independence

1778 Became the Minister to France and signed the Treaty of Alliance

1787 Signed the United States Constitution

1790 Died on April 17 in Philadelphia

I. M. Pei

I. M. Pei was born in China in 1917. When he was a child, he watched as workers constructed a 23-story building in Shanghai. How, he wondered, could such a tall building stand in a country that had so many great storms and earthquakes?

Pei loved learning about how buildings were made. He wanted to design buildings. When he was ready for college, he traveled to the United States.

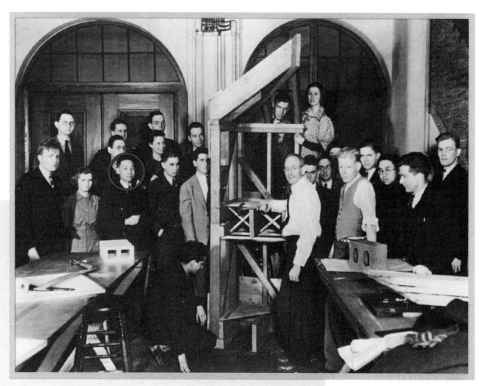

College student Pei

Shanghai, a city in China where Pei lived, in the 1920s

Architects often build models of their designs.

Pei liked the United States. When World War II started, he decided to stay in the United States. He continued to study design.

Housing in Manhattan, New York, designed by Pei

Pei designed apartments in many cities. Some apartments were for people who did not have much money. Pei always designed the best buildings he could in every community.

"I want to bring out the best in a community and contribute something of permanent value."

I. M. Pei

Pei also designed art museums. Most of his museums had huge windows that let in lots of light. Inside, round halls and stairways give visitors the feeling of fun and excitement.

Pei designed a library in honor of President John F. Kennedy. The beautiful building is made of concrete and glass and sits near Boston Harbor.

The John Fitzgerald Kennedy Library at night

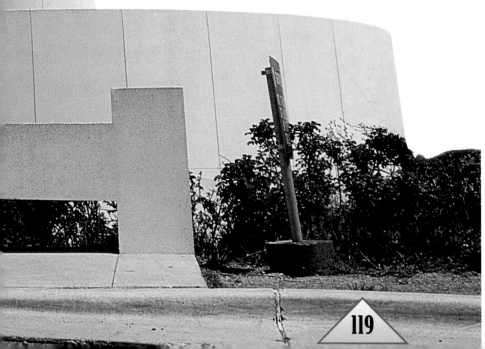

The John Fitzgerald Kennedy Library

Pei wanted buildings to fit in with the land. When he designed a science lab in the Rocky Mountains, he learned about the buildings of the Native Americans who had lived there.

"Good architecture lets nature in."

I. M. Pei

The Mesa Laboratory, shown on these pages, blends into its surroundings.

Pei designed the lab with towers that looked like some of the Native American buildings he had learned about.

In Paris, France, Pei designed part of a famous museum. People can enter the museum and go underground to all the different parts of the museum.

Pei's pyramid at the Grand Louvre Museum, Paris, France

I. M. Pei has designed concert halls, libraries, banks, science labs, hotels, office buildings, apartment buildings, and art museums. He also designed the Rock and Roll Hall of Fame in Cleveland, Ohio.

Bank of China

Rock and Roll Hall of Fame

Pei doesn't have to watch others design buildings any more. He is designing them himself!

Pei has won many awards.

Let's Explore!

This map shows only a few of Pei's buildings. In which direction would you go if you wanted to travel from the John Fitzgerald Kennedy Library in Boston, Massachusetts, to the Rock and Roll Hall of Fame in Cleveland, Ohio?

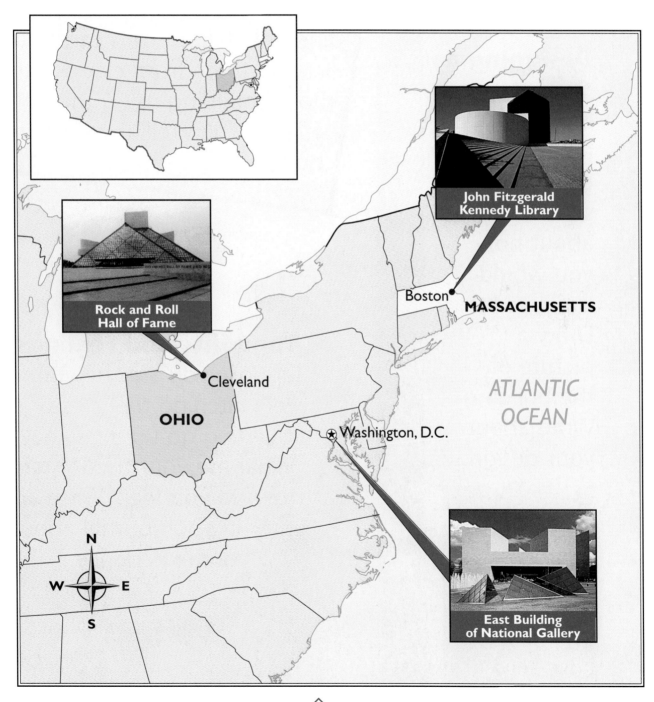

John Fitzgerald
Kennedy Library

Rock and Roll
Hall of Fame

Boston   **MASSACHUSETTS**

*ATLANTIC
OCEAN*

Cleveland

OHIO

Washington, D.C.

N
W   E
S

East Building
of National Gallery

What Do You Think?

Different Shapes

Buildings are designed using different shapes. Cut out different shapes from cardboard or form them from clay. Make a model building using the shapes. Then tell about your building.

Designing a School

Suppose you are asked to design a new school. Think about how you would like it to look. Draw a picture of the building. Write about your design.

Thoughts and Feelings

Suppose you are the young Pei watching the 23-story building go up in China. What are your thoughts? How do you feel? Write an entry in your journal about your experience.

Alike and Different

I. M. Pei designed many buildings. How are his buildings the same? How are they different?

Key Events

1917   I. M. Pei is born in China.

1940   Pei graduates from college.

1954   Pei becomes a United States citizen.

1967   Pei completes a science lab in Colorado.

1979   The John F. Kennedy Library opens in Massachusetts.

1989   Pei completes work on a museum in Paris, France.

1995   Pei designs the Rock and Roll Hall of Fame in Ohio.

Antonia Novello

In 1990 Dr. Antonia Novello was named Surgeon General. The Surgeon General is the official doctor and health expert in the United States. Antonia became the first woman and the first Hispanic to hold that job.

Justice Sandra Day O'Connor swears in Dr. Novello as her mother, husband, President Bush, and the Secretary of Health and Human Services look on.

Dr. Novello wears the uniform of vice admiral of the United States Navy as Surgeon General.

Antonia, called Tonita by her family, was born in Puerto Rico. Her father died when she was little. Antonia's mother was a teacher and principal who told Antonia how important it was to get an education.

Puerto Rico means "rich port" in Spanish. San Juan, shown here, is its capital.

Antonia was born with a medical problem. When she was growing up, she spent a lot of time in hospitals. Because of her own sickness, she decided to become a pediatrician to help other sick children.

A pediatrician is a doctor who specializes in the care and diseases of children.

Antonia applied to medical school when she was still in college. She was accepted at the University of Puerto Rico and specialized in childhood diseases.

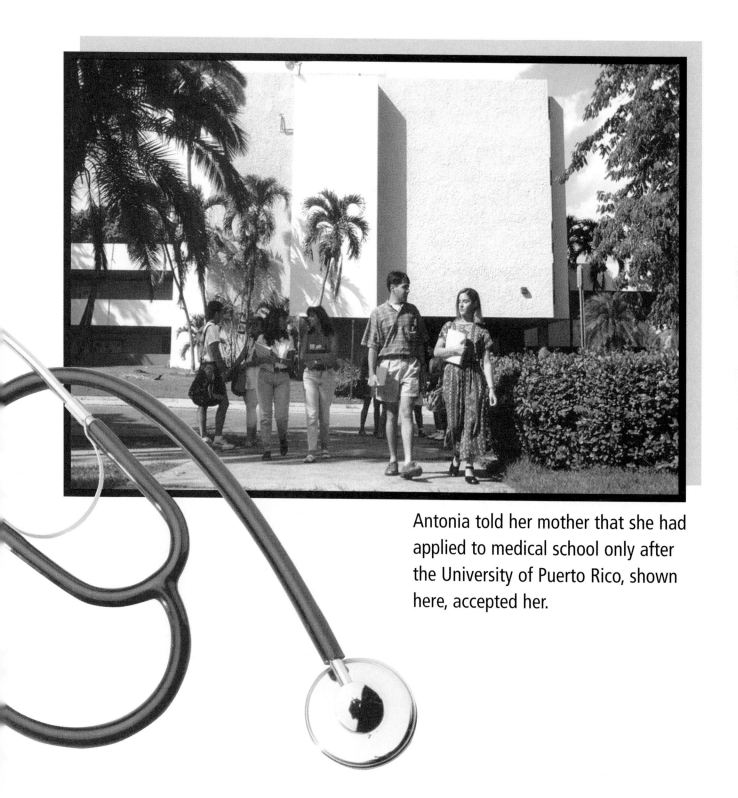

Antonia told her mother that she had applied to medical school only after the University of Puerto Rico, shown here, accepted her.

Antonia met Doctor Joseph Novello while she was in medical school. They were married right after Antonia graduated.

Dr. Joseph Novello was in the United States Navy and lived in Puerto Rico when he met Antonia.

Antonia and Joseph moved to Michigan, where she worked as an intern at a university hospital.

Antonia was named Intern of the Year at the University of Michigan.

135

Antonia and Joseph moved to Washington, D.C.
She opened her own doctor's office. After a few years,
she went to work for the United States Public Health
Service—a group that teaches people about good
health habits.

Here Dr. Novello speaks with students about the dangers of drugs.

She loved helping people to stay healthy.
Dr. Novello worked and wrote about
preventing AIDS—a very serious illness.

Dr. Novello speaks about good health for all Americans.

President Bush liked what Antonia wrote. He offered her the job of Surgeon General of the United States.

Antonia Novello and President Bush

SMOKE FREE CLASS OF 2000

Dr. Novello warned the public about the danger of smoking.

While Surgeon General, Antonia gave speeches about the dangers of drugs, alcohol, and smoking. She visited schoolchildren, telling them how to stay healthy.

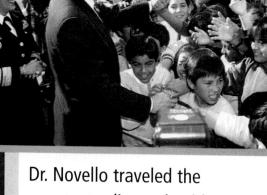

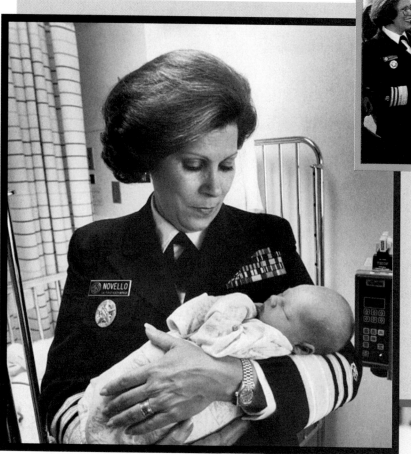

Dr. Novello traveled the country to discuss health problems. She often took time to visit sick children.

In 1993 Antonia stepped down from her job as Surgeon General. In her roles as doctor and Surgeon General, Antonia had made a difference in many people's lives.

Dr. Novello still gives speeches. She hopes that if her words make good sense, people will be willing to make good changes for healthier lives.

Let's Explore!

Antonia Novello was born in Puerto Rico. Puerto Rico is an island. She worked as Surgeon General in Washington, D.C. In which direction do you travel to get from Puerto Rico to Washington, D.C.?

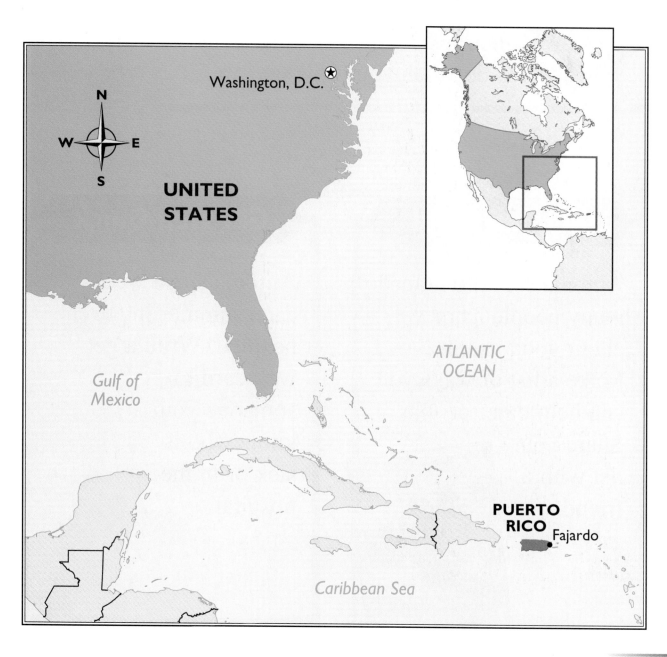

What Do You Think?

What will I be?

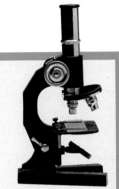

Antonia Novello knew when she was young that she wanted to be a children's doctor. What do you want to do? Write a journal entry about what you would most like to do when you grow up.

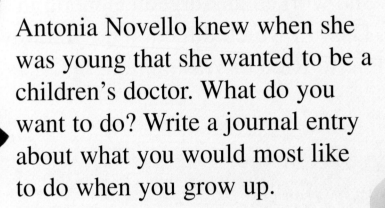

Helping Hand

Antonia Novello helped many people learn about good health. Make a list of ways you can help other people. Share your list with a friend.

Get Well Quick

Antonia spent weeks each summer in the hospital. Write a get well card to someone you know who is sick or in the hospital.

Other Female Firsts

Sandra Day O'Connor
Supreme Court Justice

Donna Shalala
Secretary of Health and Human Services

Sally Ride
First American woman in space

Janet Reno
Attorney General

Key Events

1944 Born in Puerto Rico

1965 Graduated from college

1970 Graduated from medical
school and married
Joseph Novello

Puerto Rico

1976 Started private practice
in Washington, D.C.

1978 Entered the U.S. Public
Health Service

1990 Named Surgeon General
of the United States

Capitol Building, Washington, D.C.

Frederick Douglass

Courtesy, The American Antiquarian Society, 65(bkg), 74(bc); Bettmann, 70(tc), 78(tl); The Bettmann Archive, 72(cr), 73(cl), 75(tr), 76(tr), 79(tl)(tr); Ralph J. Brunke/ASG Sherman Graphics, Inc., 78(br); The Granger Collection, New York, 65(t), 66–67, 68(tr)(bc), 69, 71(cr), 72(bl), 73(br), 74(tc), 75(b), 79(bl)(br), 80; Howard University, 71(cl), 76(bl); The Library of Congress, 68(tl); National Portrait Gallery, Smithsonian Institution/Art Resource, NY, 65(c); PhotoEdit, 75(tl); Collection of Picture Research Consultants, 66; UPI/Bettmann, 70(tl).

Abraham Lincoln

Bettmann, 89(cl); The Bettmann Archive, 84(cl), 85(br), 87(br), 89(cr), 90(tl)(b), 91(bl); ©Craig J. Brown/Liaison International, 82(c); Ralph J. Brunke/ASG Sherman Graphics, Inc., 94(tr)(b); Chicago Historical Society, 85(cl); Gamma, 96(b); The Granger Collection, New York, 83(tr), 84(br), 86(b), 87(cl), 88(tr)(cl), 91(tl); ©1994 Wesley Hitt/Liaison International, 95(tl); Courtesy of the Illinois State Historical Library, 82(b), 91(br); ©Herbert Lambs/Black Star, 81(b); The Library of Congress, 83(b); National Portrait Gallery, Smithsonian Institution/Art Resource, NY, 81(cl), 92(cl); New York Herald, 92(br); Courtesy, Meserve-Kunhardt Collection, 88(cr)(bl); ©Ken Ross/Liaison International, 95(cr); UPI/Bettmann, 81(cr), 90(tr), 95(bl).

Ben Franklin

The Bettmann Archive, 102(tl)(b), 104(b), 105, 108(b), 110(b), 111(c), 112(bkg)(tr)(bl); Courtesy, CIGNA Museum and Art Collection, 103; The Granger Collection, New York, 97, 98, 99, 100, 101, 102(r), 104(t), 106, 107, 108(t), 110(t), 112(cl); National Portrait Gallery, Smithsonian Institution/Art Resource, NY, 112(b); PhotoDisc Images ©1995 PhotoDisc, Inc., 111(tl)(cr), 112(cr).

I. M. Pei

AP/Wide World Photos, 124(bl); Bettmann, 125(c); The Bettmann Archive, 114–115; ©The Image Bank, 125(tr); ©Sandra Baker/Liaison International, 120; ©P. & G. Bowater/The Image Bank, 123(t); ©Jay Brousseau/The Image Bank, 127(cl); ©Alain Choisnet/The Image Bank, 122(t); ©Mel Digiacomo/The Image Bank, 127(b); Owen Franken/Gamma, 113; ©Jan Halaska/Photo Researchers, Inc., 127(bl); ©Armen Kachaturian/The Gamma Liaison, 128(r); ©B. Kraft/Sygma, 124(t); ©John Lamb/Tony Stone Images, 127(tl); ©MCMXC David Perry Lawrence/The Image Bank, 128(b); The MIT Museum, 115, 116; National Center for Atmospheric Research/University Corporation for Atmospheric Research/National Science Foundation, 121(t); ©Marvin E. Newman/The Image Bank, 122(b); The Image Bank, 125(b); ©Springer/Liaison International. 123(b); ©1991 Art Stein/Photo Researchers, Inc., 126(b); Ezra Stoller/©Esto, 121(b); ©1993 Joseph Szkodzinski/The Image Bank, 118–119; ©Masa Uemura/Tony Stone Images, 119; UPI/Bettmann, 114, 116–117, 124(br); ©Bill Wisser/Liaison International, 127(tr).

Antonia Novello

AP/Wide World Photos, 130(t); Made by Corel, cover wrap(bkg), 129(bkg), 142(cr); ©1991 Dennis Brack/Black Star, 139(br); ©Robert E. Daemmrich/Tony Stone Images, 132; ©Robert Frerck/Tony Stone Images, 144(t); Gamma, 143(tr); ©Dirck Halstead/The Gamma Liaison, 139(tr); ©Cynthia Johnson/The Gamma Liaison, 130(br); ©John Marshall/Tony Stone Images, 131(bl); ©J. Messerschmidt/Tony Stone Images, 131(t); University of Michigan Medical Center, 135; ©Jon Ortner/Tony Stone Images, 144(b); PhotoDisc Images ©1995 PhotoDisc, Inc., 132–133, 134(br), 142(tl)(tr)(cl); ©Photoreporters, 129, 140; Reuters/Bettmann, 143(br); ©Loren Santow/Tony Stone Images, 142(bl); UPI/Bettmann, 137, 138, 143(bl); UPR-Río Piedras Campus, 133; ©Theo Westenberger/The Gamma Liaison, 143(tl); ©Gary Williams/Gamma Liaison, 136; ©1990 Taro Yamasaki/*People Weekly,* 134(cl), 139(cl).

Illustration credits—

Shawn Banner, 126(l); Bob Lange, 31, 105, 111, 126(r); Ortelius Design, 13, 29, 45, 61, 77, 93, 125, 141; The Quarasan Group, Inc., 14, 78, 98–112(folios), 142; The Quarasan Group, Inc./Silhouettes, Dover Publications, Inc., 94; Den Schofield/Philip M. Veloric, 109.